Menai Bridge

THE ISLAND OF
ANGLESEY
COAST PATH

Mike Salter

FOLLY PUBLICATIONS

Looking down on Holyhead Harbour

ACKNOWLEDGEMENTS

Helen Thomas took the photographs on pages 3 and 7.
The other photographs are all by Mike Salter, who also drew the maps.
Thanks to the staff at Aspect Design for their help in preparing illustrations and generally assembling the artwork of the book ready for publication.

DISCLAIMER

Every effort has been made to ensure information in this book is accurate and up-to-date, but the author/publisher does not accept any responsibility for any accidents to users, nor is any responsibility accepted for any problems that might arise through any of the information given being inaccurate, incomplete or out-of-date. Please take careful note of the suggestions about outdoor safety given on page 7.

AUTHOR'S NOTES

Distances are given in miles, still the most familiar unit of measurement for most British people. Although modern Ordnance Survey maps are metric, heights and amounts of climb in this book are given in feet, mainly so as to avoid any ambiguity as to whether an m following a figure means miles or metres. The contours on the Landranger maps are at 10 metre intervals, i.e. crossing three of them means roughly 100 feet of climb.

ABOUT THE AUTHOR

Mike Salter is 53 and has been a professional author and publisher since 1988. He is particularly interested in the planning and layout of medieval buildings and has a huge collection of plans of castles and old churches he has measured during tours (mostly by bicycle and motorcycle) throughout all parts of the British Isles since 1968. Woilverhampton born and bred, Mike now lives in an old cottage beside the Malvern Hills. Since walking Land's End to John O'Groats in 2004 following his 50th birthday he has done many other long distance backpacking trails. He is a life member of both the YHA and English Heritage, and he is also a member of the Backpackers Club and the Mountain Bothies Association. His other interests include railways, board games, morris dancing and calling folk dances and playing percussion with an occasional ceilidh band.

New stone path up Holyhead Mountain

CONTENTS

INTRODUCTION

The main route of the Isle of Anglesy coast path is about 120 miles, but there are several short dead-ends which add on about four miles or so, plus there are a couple of short other suggested diversions to visit churches and other monuments which will add two or three more miles. One of the great advantages of a path around an island is that only a single Ordnance Survey map is required for eight to ten days' walking. Much of the coastline, especially around the southern corner, is flat and low-lying. There are a number of short climbs here and there but the only really mountainous sections lie west of Cemaes and Holyhead respectively. There are several sections where the alternatives are shingle at high tide and firm sand at low tide, but there is hardly any boggy ground and in hot weather trekking sandals are a viable alternative to boots. One or two short sections may be overgrown in summer and there are two sections where gorse bushes slightly obscure the path. There are comparatively few stiles, and instead there are a large number of kissing gates. Unfortunately some of these, including a number which are obviously brand new, don't allow enough space for anyone of large stature or even a thin person wearing a large backpack, so some climbing may occasionally be required.

The official start and finish of the walk is in St Cybi's churchyard in Holyhead, and this lies within a third of a mile of a station with trains arriving and departing roughly hourly for most of the day. With a route that forms a circle the direction of travel doesn't make much difference in terms of facing the sun and wind, but going clockwise gives a spectacular finish coming into Holyhead over Holyhead Mountain. Stations at Llanfair P.G., Bodorgan, and Rosneigr all lie within two thirds of a mile of the path and make possible starting points but they are served by less trains, especially important if you are finishing on a Sunday, when there's just one morning train stopping at these lesser stations.

The island is very geared to the needs of holiday-makers and B&Bs are plentiful. The longest section without B&Bs on or close to the path is the 16 miles between Llanfachraeth and Cemaes, but you could divert inland for just over a mile to Llanfaethlu. Hiring a cottage or caravan and using buses to reach different sections of the path should also be viable. There are no youth hostels and there's only one independant hostel (Cerrig-yr-Adar, at SH 278752, Rhoscolyn, at the south end of Holy Island), but campsites are plentiful, especially around Benllech. Shops are frequent, so you shouldn't need to carry more than a day or two's food, and there are quite a number of take-away food places. Holyhead, Amlwch, Benllech and Menai Bridge are the only places on the coast where you are likely to find banks, pharmacies or places to buy fuel for camping stoves.

Beaumaris Castle

There are plenty of places where you can camp out wild near the shore without any facilities, although it isn't encouraged by the authorities and is against bylaws in several places, particularly on National Trust lands and beside county council car-parks. Its unlikely you'll be arrested for camping, unless you are causing damage, noise or pollution, but you could be moved on. It is legal to stop for rest or refreshment whilst walking along a right-of-way but there is no right to erect any sort of shelter, however temporary. The basic rule about wild camping is to be discreet. Use a tent with a flysheet of a colour that blends with the surroundings, pitch fairly late and leave early. Don't camp in large groups, light fires, leave rubbish or make noise, and don't camp close to, or within sight of, roads, farms and houses unless you've got permission from the landowner. There are plenty of public toilets on Anglesey and almost all have proper taps and washbasins rather than wall-units, but nearly all of them are locked by around 5.30pm. Some were not open at all even in July and about half are seasonal, being locked throughout the winter months, so campers may occasionally have to carry drinking water a fair distance as it isn't safe to drink out of any of the streams.

Several sections of the route are permissive paths rather than rights of way. They may be closed at certain times of year, eg to allow birds to nest or for shooting or other special activities. Other sections of path may be submerged by very high tides. Usually there's a road alternative, but this may not be fully signed and may add some mileage.

ENVIRONMENTAL IMPACT

Basically: Leave nothing but footprints, take nothing but photographs & memories. So:
Don't leave any litter, even biodegradable material such as fruit cores and skins.
Don't pick flowers or damage trees & plants, except where necessary to clear a path.
Don't make lots unecessary noise, especially when passing through farmyards.
Don't get so close to animals that they become stressed and abandon their young.
Don't stray from the path on sections where you can clearly see its intended route.
Don't touch farming or forestry equipment, crops, timber stacks or building materials.
Leave all gates as you find them, whether open or closed.
Be discreet if wild camping (see page 5), and guard against all risk of starting fires.

Use public toilets where possible. If you have to go outdoors make sure you are at least 30m from running water and bury excrement in a small hole where it will decompose quicker. Do not bury tampons or sanitary towels. You will have to carry these out. Ideally you should also do this with toilet paper also, since it doesn't decompose quickly and will blow around if dug up by animals.

If you are taking a dog with you it will need to be on a short lead at all times since there are many sections where there are sheep, cows or breeding grounds for wild birds. Also you will need to think carefully about where you will be able to stay. Dogs are specifically banned from some of the beaches during the summer months and there are sections of permissive path where there are restrictions on dogs.

NAVIGATIONAL AIDS

The Ordnance Survey Landranger map 114 should be adequate for the walk, which is mostly fairly well signed. You should carry a compass and know how to use it together with the map but its unlikely that you'll need to do this on Anglesey , as there aren't long sections of bare moorland where you can get very lost.

A useful item is a Global Positioning System. You can check your speed and distance, and time travelled, but best of all it will give you a grid reference accurate to a few feet. Those who like treasure hunting can additionally use the unit to find geocaches (website details given on page 20), of which there are many along the route. GPS units use up batteries quickly, and nead a clear view of the sky, so they are not so good in forests.

Thomas Telford's bridge over the Menai Straits

Remains of a rectangular hut on Holyhead Mountain

OUTDOOR SAFETY

Careful walking and footwear that gives a reasonable grip is needed on some sections of the path where there are steep drops. There are a few sections with unfenced sheer drops, although these are mostly very short and in most cases the drop is not very far.

Sort out any problems with feet, footwear or socks immediately. Make sure you carry enough dry clothes to remain warm even in the most wet and stormy conditions, and carry enough food and drink so that you don't have to rush unduly or take risks. Take care not to be cut-off by the tide on beaches. If in doubt stay above high-tide level. Be realistic when estimating distances. Cliff-top paths meandering around headlands and inlets go further than they look on the map. Don't expect to make more than three miles an hour even if fit, lightly loaded and weather conditions are favourable. Averaging two miles an hour will be good going for a party of people carrying camping equipment.

Llangadwaladwr Church

ROUTE DESCRIPTION

HOLYHEAD - LLANFACHRAETH

The official new start/finish board of the Isle of Anglesey Coast Path lies just inside the southern gateway of St Cybi's churchyard at SH 247826, in the middle of Holyhead, and the mileages are calculated from that point, but if you've arrived by train with all the supplies you need for a day or two then you can start walking direct from the station, which lies a third of a mile further south.

The churchyard walls are those of a small 3rd century Roman fort with circular corner turrets. It protected a command base for a small fleet which was then able to anchor directly below the east side, which seems to have been left unwalled. In the SW corner is the nave of the 14th century Eglwys Y Bedd or Chapel of The Dead, made into a school in the 18th century. St Cybi's Church has a 17th century tower abutting the west wall of the Roman fort. The chancel has 13th century walling but it and the south chapel were mostly rebuilt in 1877-9. The embattled transepts and the aisled nave with a fan-vaulted south porch and polygonal stair-turret are mostly late medieval work of c1480-1520.

Meths and camping gas are available from a hardware shop not far beyond the north gate of the churchyard, whilst the main street to the south contains a range of supermarkets, pharmacies, other shops, and cafes, pubs and restaurants.

After passing Holyhead Station the coast path goes round two low headlands. The first has a housing estate backing onto it (not quite as bad as it sounds) and gives close-up views of the Irish ferries docking opposite. The second is the Penrhos Country Park, with some woodland, duckponds, signboards and toilets at the south end, after which you cross over from Holy Island to the Anglesey mainland on a causeway which also carries the A5 and the dual carriageway A55, plus the railway. At the east end the path drops onto a shingle beach., from which there is a path into Newlands Park at SH 291805. If a mile of walking on shingle isn't to your taste then stay beside A5 until you reach the road running along the SE side of the housing estate of Newlands Park. You'll need the road that runs from it eastwards to join A5025 at Llanynghenedl since the coast path runs to a dead end on the south side of an estuary, The path shown on the OS map joining it to the road doesn't actually exist anymore, and the only through route is by going a mile along the lane now marked as a cycletrack, and then another mile along the A5025 to Llanfachraeth, 7m from Caer Gybi, which has a pub and a small corner shop.

Caer Gybi Church

At the staggered crossroads in Llanfachraeth turn left down a dead-end lane for a third of a mile, then join a path which alternates running along the shore for short sections with inland cut-offs through meadows. Pass over bracken-covered low dunes, over a causeway and then past a ruined house to join a longer (1 mile) section along a shore, where walking on the sands is possible at low tide. The path briefly swings inland on a lane towards Llanfwrog, then turns left up the drive to Penial Dowyn, which is bypassed by a route through meadows and up over a small hill. At the top the route down from the stile may be overgrown with tall grass in high summer, but there's a new track (not a right-of-way) as a alternative just SW of the field boundary. The route then follows tracks leading between two large caravan sites (one allows camping) to Porth Tywyn-Mawr

Follow the track east of Porth Tywyn-Mawr to Trefadog, beyond which a new section of permissive path rounds a headland to rejoin the track, and then tarmac road to Borthwen. Beyond lies a mile of path on National Trust land leading past Grugmor to Porth Swtan, 14m from Caer Gybi, where there's a carpark with toilets and a cafe.

The next section is a heritage coast, more rugged and demanding for walkers. The route keeps fairly close to the cliff-edge for the two miles to the rock-arch and island at Ynys y Fydlyn. although in places there's a bewildering selection of alternative paths, some created by grazing stock. The inland lake here is now almost dry and the woodland doesn't really encroach on the route in the way the OS map suggests. Over Carmel Head there isn't really one obvious main path. Head for the chimney and then pass to the northern and lower down of the two tall markers for shipping. Further east the route has gates at the head of each inlet but not much actual path either round the headlands or cutting across their necks.

East of the tiny bay of Hen Borth take the path across a meadow to the lovely little church of Llanrhwydrys at SH 322932. A round-arched Norman doorway leads into a part of the nave now covered by a gallery, and the long narrow chancel is 13th century. Another path from the church leads into Tyn-Llan farmyard, and another path from the farm lane leads northwards back to the coastal path.

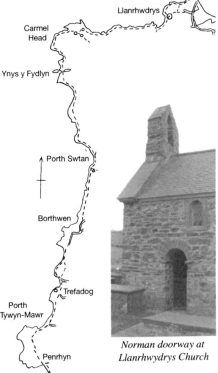

Norman doorway at Llanrhwydrys Church

Just north of the high walled garden is a tiny bridge (covered by high tides) leading onto the shingle-covered causeway across Cemlyn Bay, There's a bird reserve behind the causeway so apart from tidal restrictions walkers are asked not to use this route during the nesting season, hence the alternative route via roads inland, adding about a third of a mile. Further east the route rounds the next headland but beyond Cestyll it curves round the edge of a wooded garden and then heads inland to avoid the power station. You then enter the power station grounds on a tarmac road only to be signposted off on a path meandering through woodlands immediately east of the power station. There's no longer a signposted route onto gorse-covered Wylfa Head (although there is public access), and the route crosses a field to run round a small inlet on the south side of Cemaes Bay, and then runs into the village of Cemaes itself, 23m from Caer Gybi, where there are several shops, pubs, accommodation and two sets of toilets (both out of use in 2006 through vandalism).

The coast-path route through Cemaes is not clearly signed but you'll pick it up from the espanade east of the stream. After a mile it passes the a church associated with St Patrick at Llanbadrig. This building contains an early carved stone and a Norman font, although the building itself is 14th century with a 16th century chancel and 19th century windows. The next four miles are scenic and have some steep climbs and descents with long flights of new steps. There are interesting remains of former industries such as a brickworks on the west side of Porth Wen, and a chimney and ruin at Porth Llanlleiana, above which is a folly gazebo. Apart from cutting off one headland north of the brickworks the path closely follows the rugged coastline. There's a shop at the resort of Bull Bay, 28m from Caer Gybi.

The coast-path doesn't go through the centre of the industrial town of Amlwch, noted for its copper mines, which lies two thirds of a mile inland, although NE of the town it does sweep inland to avoid a chemical works before going around the head of the small but once very busy Amlwch Port, the history of which is described on signboards. However most walkers will probably need to use the shops. Just SW of the 19th century church is the only large supermarket near the coastpath apart from those at Holyhead.

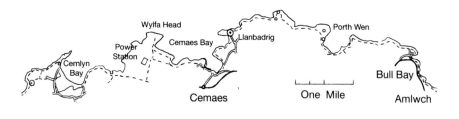

Porth Wen, showing the ruined brickworks

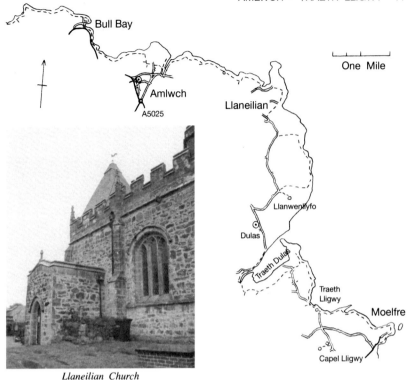

Llaneilian Church

From Amlwch Port the path follows the coast for two miles to Llaneilian, 31m from Caer Gybi, where the church (kept locked) has a Norman west tower and an embattled nave and chancel of the 15th century. A porch was added in the 16th century and in 1614 a short passage was added to link the chancel to a formerly detached 14th or 15th century chapol of St Filian on a different orientation, probably the site of an early cell.

A mile after the short diversion inland to Llaneilian church the path heads SW steeply up to meet a road, since there's a mile of coast lacking any form of path. After half a mile on the road the path descends back to the coast, only to climb back up again after a mile, so you may find it easier simply to stay on the road (a quiet winding lane with good views) to the corner at SH 482902. From here a track leads down to the overgrown remains of the old church (probably 16th century) of LLanwenllyfo. After returning to the corner continue down the road and turn left at a T-junction to pass the 19th centuy church on the way back to the coast path around Traeth Dulas. There's a new water tap near the gateway of the churchyard of the newer church, which contains a fine set of 16th century stained glass windows brought here from Flanders, and a brass of 1609 depicting Marcellie Lloyd and one of her two husbands moved here from the old church.

There's a track by the shore of Traeth Dulas, but at low tide there's sand to walk on. After crossing the stream a path goes through to the farm-lane to Pentre Eirianell. You may be able to use the track through the farmyard, but strictly speaking the coast path goes along A5025 for a short distance to a pub. Beyond the route traverses meadows high above Traeth Dulas, although there's little actual path to follow. It then descends to the coast at Penrhyn.

There's a possible short diversion inland down the road just east of the toilets at Traeth Lligwy to see the ruined Capel Lligwy, which is Norman and 14th century, with a tiny added 16th century south chapel. Just south of the chapel a path leads west from the road to Din Lligwy, a 4th century walled pentagonal enclosure about 150ft long containing remains of several rectangular and circular huts. Also in the vicinity is a neolithic burial chamber created over a natural fissure in the ground.

The coast path continues past a small inlet and round a headland and then joins the A5108 for a short section through Moelfre, 40m from Caer Gybi, where there are shops. SE of Nant Bychan the route traverses two meadows to reach a carpark with toilets at Traeth Bychan. Steps up through woodland then lead south. For most of the next mile from the headland down to Benllech the path is a narrow passage between tall hedges, and inland from it there's a continuous series of holiday chalets and camp sites. Benllech, 43m from Caer Gybi, is very much a holiday resort, and has several shops, including a pharmacy. A mile beyond is Red Wharf Bay, where there's a car park, pub, campsite and toilets.

Part of the path around Red Wharf Bay is actually on the shore and you can walk on the sands at low tide. East of where the path touches a corner of a road at SH 553801 the route follows the top of a shore defence wall for 300 yards. This section has vertical drops on both sides and may be unsuitable for dogs or small children. Further on there's another set of toilets and at SH 574808 is the church of Llanddona, which was entirely rebuilt in 1873 except for the 15th century south doorway. Either turn left beside the church and left again higher up the hill, or go back 100yards to take the path heading north along the shore.

At Pentrellwyn the path follows a track north for a short distance before climbing up to pick up another path around the northern slopes of Bwrdd Arthur. Opposite where a path heads east off the track there's an access across a field to the 15th century church of Llanfihangel Din Sylwy (kept locked), 50m from Caer Gybi. After a third of a mile the path leads to a road through Mariandyrys. Follow it for a mile, ignoring a road on each side, before taking a path on the left. This leads past a sequence of farmhouses and cottages before leading through to another road. Beyond Pentir there's a path leading beside the northern side of the wall of Penmon deerpark. After going through a narrow belt of woodland the path heads east to Trwyn Penmon, a headland pointing out towards Puffin Island, a bird santuary with early monastic remains. The toilets shown on the OS map actually belong to a cafe, and are not for general public use.

Follow the unfenced road west for a mile to Penmon Priory, 54m from Caer Gybi. There's an exhibition of rubbings of early crosses and inscribed stones on Anglesey in the nave of the church dating from the 1140s. The transepts and central tower are later Norman additions, although the north transept and the more spacious 13th century chancel have been mostly rebuilt. There's a sheela-na-gig or nude female exhibitionist figure on the south transept internal west wall. South of the chancel lay a cloister (now a garden serving an inhabited house adjoining the south transept) and there are ruins of a 13th century range which served the Augustinian canons both as a refectory and domitory, whilst a 16th century building adjoins it to the east. Not far NE is a garden containing a holy well of St Seriol and the footings of a hermit's hut, and there's a square dovecot crowned with a cupola built c1600 by Sir Richard Bulkeley.

Penmon Priory

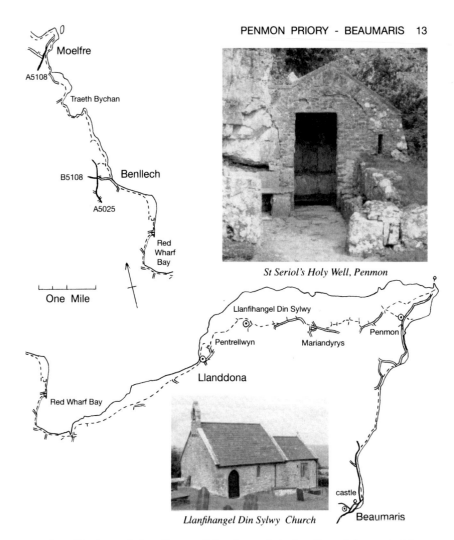

St Seriol's Holy Well, Penmon

Llanfihangel Din Sylwy Church

A road leads south from Penmon Priory for a mile before the path leaves to follow the shore. It briefly rejoins the road as far as a car park, then there's a section over a mile long on shingle along the shore. The path joins B5109 a mile north of Beaumaris, but the last section into the village. is over two fields above the shore.

Beaumaris is 58m from Caer Gybi via the coast path and is noted for its fine castle begun by Edward I in 1295 as a response to a recent Welsh revolt, during which the incomplete castle at Caernarfon at the other end of the Menai Straits had been captured. The castle has a massively-walled square inner ward with four circular corner towers, D-shaped towers in the middle of two sides (one contains a chapel), and two huge twin-towered gatehouses. It was left incomplete in the 1320s with the towers still not raised above the main wallwalk as intended and the inner parts of the southern gatehouse never completed. Completely surrounding this inner ward is an octagonal outer ward with many circular towers fronting onto a partly restored water-filled moat. This concentric outer ward also has an incomplete gatehouse on the northern side. It encloses a small dock on the south side. Beaumaris was the centre of English influence on Anglesey and has a very English-looking early 14th century church partly remodelled with a new chancel c1500. It contains several interesting monuments including a brass of the 1530s and a coffin-lid with a half effigy of Princess Joan, an illegitimate daughter of King John who was married to Llewelyn ap Gruffydd, then ruler of Gwynedd. The village has several shops, a chip shop, and toilets.

Beaumaris Church

From Beaumaris the path follows A 545 for half a mile, then takes a lane on the right leading up past a cemetery and under a private drive in a belt of woodland. After half a mile a path cuts a corner off through to a lane which is quiet at first but which leads to a wider and busier road serving an estate, and having a shop beside it. There are other shops in the village of Menai Bridge, where, after joining A545 for a short section, the route follows quiet back streets along the shore and then goes under Thomas Telford's celebrated suspension bridge of 1818-26, which is 62m from Caer Gybi, roughly halfway round. The main span is 580ft wide and is tall enough for ships with 100ft high masts.

Not far beyond the bridge there's a causeway across to a small island upon which is the church of Llandysilio, a simple rectangle with an old roof structure. Although at low tide you could sneak along the shore the path officially goes inland beyond the island and follows A5 for a third of a mile before a permissive path leads down to the shore and across a meadow. The path then goes through a short section of woodland and climbs up under the piers of the Pont Brittania, rebuilt as a combined road and rail bridge, using the old piers of George Stephenson's tubular railway bridge destroyed by fire.

The short section of path through the churchyard of Llanfair Pwllgwyngyll (known on Anglesey as Llanfair P.G.) and out to the shore beside a staue of Lord Nelson is a dead end unless its low tide and you can cope with a difficult section along a shingle-shore. The problem here is that the Marquess of Anglesey's house of Plas Newydd lies by the shore a mile and half further along, and although the house is opened to the public by the National Trust, the marquess still resides there and consequently there's no public path through the walled grounds. The alternative is to follow A5 for half a mile, passing a a statue of 1860 to the first Marquess on a 90ft high column on a rock (open to the public), then to walk a mile along the A4080, which has no pavement or proper verge. A path then leads off on the right. There's a water tap in the meadow just before the paths divide and you go left over a stile. When you reach a building go right and then left to reach a section of wolodland path with a wall on the south side. Cross a meadow, pass another tap in the passage of the farmyard you go through to reach a road, and then follow the road to a crossroads on A4080. This section is not officially part of the signed coast path. Cross over and go down a lane a mile to Y Felinheli, 67m from Caer Gybi.

Since Y Felinheli is a dead end you'll need to retrace your steps inland a short way to pick up a road heading SW. At a T-junction go left and then immediately right (its almost a crossroads) onto a track out to the shore for half a mile before a track climbs up to a junction beside Llanidan Church, a semi ruined structure in private grounds by a house. You'll be able to see part of the 15th century arcade over the boundary wall. From the junction by the church go west for a short distance to pick up a path on the left unless you need the shop, pub or toilets in the village of Brynsiencyn, in which case ignore the path.

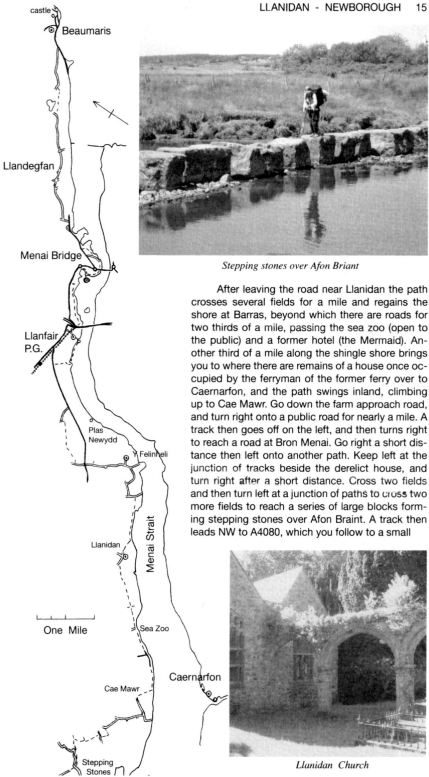

Stepping stones over Afon Briant

After leaving the road near Llanidan the path crosses several fields for a mile and regains the shore at Barras, beyond which there are roads for two thirds of a mile, passing the sea zoo (open to the public) and a former hotel (the Mermaid). Another third of a mile along the shingle shore brings you to where there are remains of a house once occupied by the ferryman of the former ferry over to Caernarfon, and the path swings inland, climbing up to Cae Mawr. Go down the farm approach road, and turn right onto a public road for nearly a mile. A track then goes off on the left, and then turns right to reach a road at Bron Menai. Go right a short distance then left onto another path. Keep left at the junction of tracks beside the derelict house, and turn right after a short distance. Cross two fields and then turn left at a junction of paths to cross two more fields to reach a series of large blocks forming stepping stones over Afon Braint. A track then leads NW to A4080, which you follow to a small

Llanidan Church

Remains of Llys Rhosyr

The path goes straight on when the main road turns right at the roundabout, but there are several reasons for staying on the A-road for the half mile into Newborough, which is 75m from Caer Gybi going clockwise around the Anglesey coast path, and is a planned settlement of the early 14th century, with a church of that period and later (much rebuilt) lying to the WSW. The village has a pub and several shops. Just SW of the church are remains of Llys Rhosyr, a palace or manor house of the 13th century princes of Gwynedd. Recently exposed and conserved are the footings of a hall, two other blocks and part of the boundary wall. From here you can follow the road past the campsite and then just after the barrier pick up a track on the left through Newborough Forest. You'll rejoin the coast path, which goes down the outside of the east boundary of the forest, at the carpark amongst the dunes by the shore, where there are toilets.

Beyond the carpark the official path goes west a bit inland, behind the coastal dunes, but it's easier, except at high tide, to walk over the sands to the approach track to the tidal island of LLanddwyn. A path down the spine of the island leads past the remains of a cruciform 16th century church to a former lighthouse (see front cover picture), and there's a row of cottages, two of which contain an exhibition. Note that camping isn't allowed on the island.

Pick up the path over dunes on the northern side of the access to the island. On reaching a track turn right and then after a short distance go left to regain the official route of the coast path. Most of the next three miles is in forest, except for a short section along the shore. The path comes alongside A 4080 and then crosses a causeway over to Maltreath, 85m from Caer Gybi, where there are a few shops and a pub.

The Cwningar headland between Malltreath Sands and Traeth Mawr lacks public paths so the coastal path remains inland in this section after crossing over the dead-end road leading SW out of Maltreath. It comes out on another dead-end road, which is followed up the hill to meet A4080. Through the village of Hamon the main road has pavements. After half a mile it reaches the church of Llangadwaladr, which has a 13th century north doorway and an ancient carved stone. It also has a very fancy south chapel dated 1661 over its west doorway.

Take a path leading west just south of the church. It crosses two fields to reach the empty house of Bont-faen, then there are two more fields to cross to reach Llwynysgaw. Instead of joining the road by the church take the path heading NW to reach a road across the Tywyn Aberffraw dunes. An alternative to using the road is a path through dunes round three sides of a square. This however adds another mile to the distance to the village of Aberffraw, which is 90m from Caer Cybi. The village has several shops, a cafe and toilets. The church to the SW is a double-naved structure, mostly 16th century with 19th century features, although parts of the south and west walls are Norman. Nearby lay the principal palace or llys of the princes of Gwynedd, but nothing remains of it.

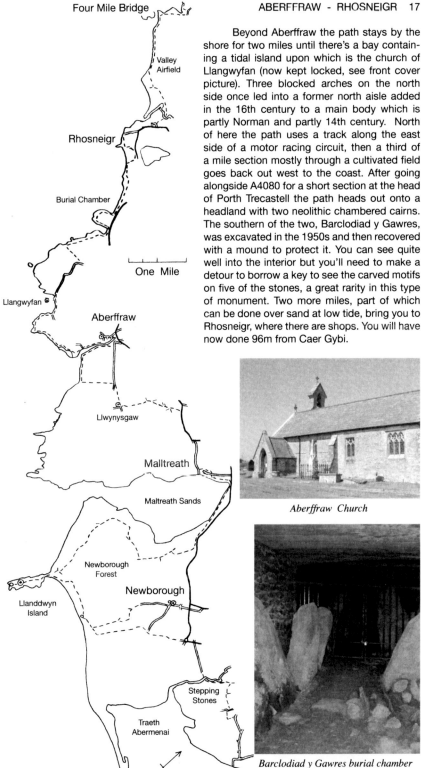

Four Mile Bridge

Valley Airfield

Rhosneigr

Burial Chamber

One Mile

Llangwyfan

Aberffraw

Llwynysgaw

Malltreath

Maltreath Sands

Newborough Forest

Newborough

Llanddwyn Island

Stepping Stones

Traeth Abermenai

Beyond Aberffraw the path stays by the shore for two miles until there's a bay containing a tidal island upon which is the church of Llangwyfan (now kept locked, see front cover picture). Three blocked arches on the north side once led into a former north aisle added in the 16th century to a main body which is partly Norman and partly 14th century. North of here the path uses a track along the east side of a motor racing circuit, then a third of a mile section mostly through a cultivated field goes back out west to the coast. After going alongside A4080 for a short section at the head of Porth Trecastell the path heads out onto a headland with two neolithic chambered cairns. The southern of the two, Barclodiad y Gawres, was excavated in the 1950s and then recovered with a mound to protect it. You can see quite well into the interior but you'll need to make a detour to borrow a key to see the carved motifs on five of the stones, a great rarity in this type of monument. Two more miles, part of which can be done over sand at low tide, bring you to Rhosneigr, where there are shops. You will have now done 96m from Caer Gybi.

Aberffraw Church

Barclodiad y Gawres burial chamber

From the shops at Rhosneigr follow the main road for half a mile before taking a lane on the left. Turn right off the lane onto a track down to a bridge. A path then leads over dunes and eventually comes out on Traeth Crigyll a short distance before you turn the corner round into Traeth Cwmyran, where at low tide there's a walk of over a mile along the sands until a track leads NE for half a mile, This is a noisy section since there will be jet fighters doing circuits around the adjacent Valley Airfield for much of the day.

When the track reaches a carpark at the end of a road take the path following the shore. After half a mile cut inland, turn left a short distance on a road, and then take a path on the left out to the shore again. You may find the next bit overgrown with gorse. The path hugs the shore of a small creek. Shortly after the ford there's an overgrown stile leading to a path off to the right across a field to the church of Llanfair yn Neubyll, a 14th century single chamber with the roof structure partly original. From the church head up to the farm and go down its lane to the road. Turn right and then left down a track after a quarter of a mile to regain the coast-path. After another mile, and having cut off one or two small headlands, you'll reach Four Mile Bridge to cross onto Holy Island, where there's a small shop. Caer Gybi is now another 19m away.

South of the bridge the path follows the shore for a while, then swings westwards to meet a road. After a third of a mile there's a new permissive path only open from Feb to Sept, through marshland on the fringe of the Bodior estate. This leads to a track heading SW to the ruined house of Bryn y bar. A path across a meadow and through woodland then leads to the shore at Silver Bay. The path stays close to the shore for a mile, and then goes round Borthwen. West of here the path climbs to 200ft and passes the holy well of St Gwenfaen out to Rhoscolyn Head. The next section, past a succession of small rocky bays, is quite scenic, but its followed by two miles of road walking, along a lane to meet B4545, through Treaddur, and then another lane off to the left, and this section is entirely flanked by houses.

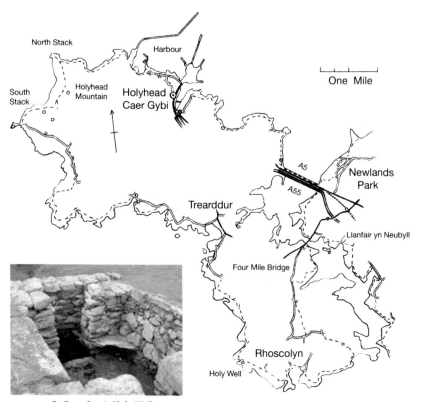

St Gwenfaen's Holy Well

On the side of Holyhead Mountain

There are bits of path round several of the tiny headlands beside the road leading out of Trearddur, but they are more trouble than they are worth and only after a mile is there a useful section of actual coastal path leading round to the toilets at Porth Dafarch. The path then leaves at a road junction, beside which is an ancient hut circle in a field. After two thirds of a mile the path passes opposite to a fort on a detached piece of headland, almost an island. After another mile and half you pass down the farm lane of Gors-goch to a road, although a new path alongside has been created here to avoid much road-walking. At the road junction turn left towards South Stack. NE of the road are a group of huts amongst the bracken, marked on the map 'Cytiau Gwyddelod', which means Irish-mens' Huts, although there is no evidence that these two thousand year old huts are in fact associated with the Irish. The circular huts were residential and the rectangular ones were for storage or industrial purposes. This important site is in the care of Cadw.

The official coast path visits both the South Stack and North Stack, the two head-lands of this spectacular upland forming a fitting climactic finish to the walk, but it is well worth the diversion to go to the summit of Holyhead Mountain, 700ft high, on the west side of which are remains of the drystone wall of an early fort. There's a lot of impres-sive new pathwork here and one lengthy section above the coast passes a vaulted hut rather like an early hermit's cell. After descending to sea-level again you simply follow the shore, first by path, then on a road, back to the north gate of the the fort of Caer Gybi.

Wall of the Roman Fort of Caer Gybi

FURTHER READING

Royal Commission on Ancient and Historical Monuments Inventory for Anglesey.
The Old Parish Churches of North Wales, Mike Salter, 1993 (see list opposite)
The Castles of North Wales, Mike Salter, 1997 (see list opposite)

USEFUL WEBSITES AND OTHER INFORMATION

www.backpackersclub.co.uk - Club for those interested in backpacking in the UK.
www.campingandcaravanningclub.co.uk - Join to obtain details of extra camp sites.
www.geocaching.com   - Finding caches using a Global Positioning System
www.ldwa.org.uk   - The Long Distance Walkers Association.
www.IndependentHostelGuide - Guide to independent hostels, new edition each year.
www.nationaltrail.co.uk   - Details of long-distance trails in UK.
www.traveline.org.uk   - Travel information throughout the UK
www.yha.org.uk   - The Youth Hostels Association of England and Wales.
National Rail Enquiries: 08457 48 49 50.   For buses ring Traveline: 0870 608 2 608
Tourist Offices: Bangor 01248 352786   bangor.tic@gwynedd.gov.uk
     Caernarfon 01286 672232   caernarfon.tic@gynedd.gov.uk
     Holyhead 01407 762622   Llanfairpwllgwyngyll 01248 713177
All Youth Hostels in Britain are open to non-members - at a small aadditional price.
    There are no youth hostels on Anglesey, but there are many around Snowdonia
    The nearest youth hostel to Anglesey is Bangor 0870 770 5686 bangor@yha.org.uk
Maps can be obtained through the Backpackers Club at a substantially reduced price.
The Backpackers Club provides members with info on farm and wild camping places.
Members of the Backpackers Club and the Long Distance Walkers Association obtain
    discounts on equipment from certain shops. Enquire for details.
In addition to the churches on or near the route already described the churches of
    Llanfairynghorny (SH 327909) and Llanfechnell (SH 370012) are of some interest.
    Both lie in the NW part of Anglesey. Penmynydd Church (SH 5177750) contains two
    monuments, one a tomb of c1385 transferred from nearby Llanfaes Friary. South of
    this church is Plas Penmynydd, seat of the ancestors of the Tudor monarchs.

Newborough Church